Utah
SEX AND TRAVEL GUIDE

CALVIN GRONDAHL

SIGNATURE BOOKS
1993

Cover design by Brian Bean

———————

Composed and printed in the United States of America.
Printed on acid free paper.
© 1993 by Signature Books, Inc. All rights reserved.
Signature Books is a registered trademark of Signature Books, Inc.

97   96   95   94   93   6   5   4   3   2   1

———————

Library Of Congress Cataloging-in-Publication Data
Grondahl, Calvin.
Utah : sex and travel guide / by Calvin Grondahl.
p.   cm.
Cartoons.
ISBN 1-56085-041-8
1. Utah—Social life and customs—Caricatures and cartoons.
2. Family—Utah—Caricatures and cartoons. 3. American wit and
humor, Pictorial.   I. Title.
F827.G77   1993
979.2—dc20   93-40831
CIP

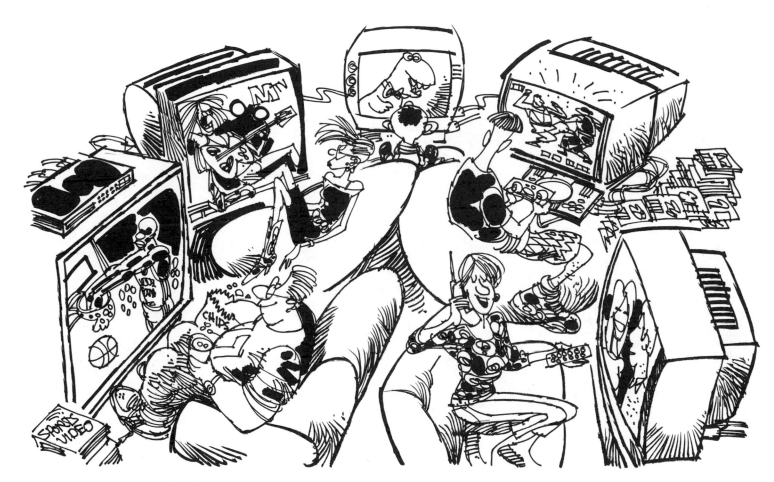

"We've moved all our televisions into one room so we could spend more time together."

"Teenagers, a new Stephen King novel. Thank you, Doris."

"*Mommy Divorces Daddy,* the story book, coloring book, video tape, and CD."

"OK, I'll talk. Just don't change your kid in here!"

"And this is rest stop 12 of 36 on our trip between Salt Lake and Bryce Canyon."

"It's our daughter. She wants us to babysit for her. . . . Floor It, George!"

"I think your mother finally cleaned your room for you."

"Was it one of those days again?"

Utah Family Disturbance

"It's the only place where her dreams have ever come true."

"Disney World with Dad. . . . Then next week Disney movie with Mom . . .
Seaworld with Dad. . . . Then Captain's Seafood with Mom."

"I want a divorce . . . I want a divorce . . . I want a divorce . . . I want a divorce . . ."

"I need more out of life than model railroading."

"Sorry, but I never go anywhere without my emotional baggage."

"Where's your bowling ball?"

"She says thanks for coming, but she can't live by a schedule."

"I told you I like to drive through the desert with the top off."

"Try page 232, second from the top. It's always worked on me before."

"He used to ski with God, but God couldn't keep up."

"So much for the painless divorce."

"Don't say it."

"We could try the back seat of the car."

"It was an accident. Your mother slipped during one of her
many lectures on my housekeeping"

"How come *we* never hold hands?"

Liberty Park Expedition

"Well, when you have eight children and only one bathroom . . ."

"Everyone drop your pants and pass them to the brother on the left."

"Son, it's not your fault you lost. . . . It's my fault. Something I did or didn't do."

"Harold, look at the tattoo our beautiful boy just got."

"Nice car. Did I mention I have five kids?"

"It worked . . . I feel pregnant already."

"You can have the house, cars, boat, . . . but not my season tickets."

"Is that our satellite dish?"

"Have you been keeping track of the contractions for me?"

Utah's only form of legalized gambling.

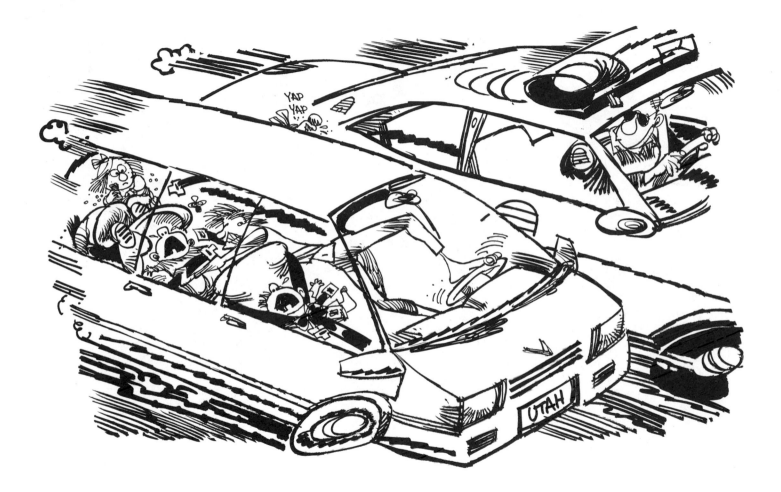

"Dad, can we raise the basket?"

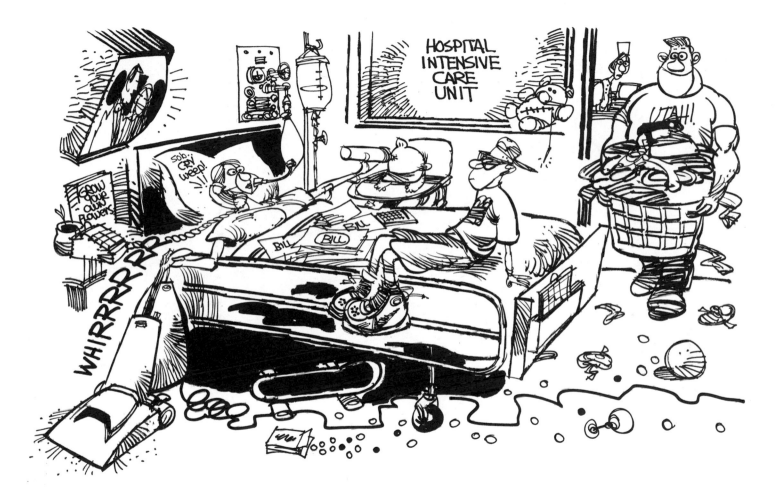

"Everybody stand back. . . . My hair is just right."

"I did that one for you and this one for me."

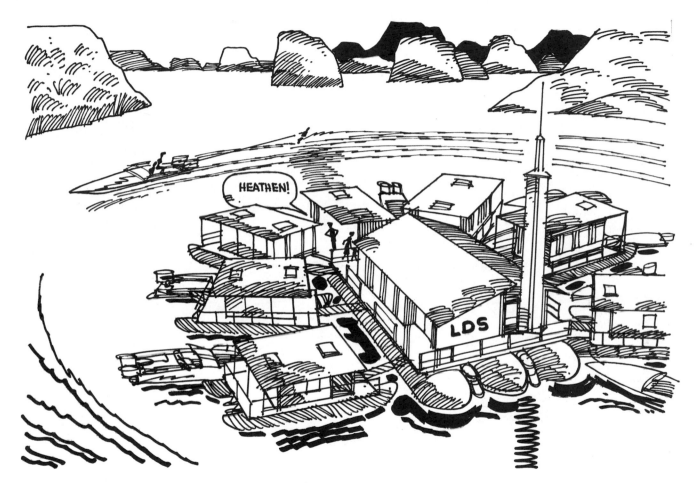

Sunday on Lake Powell

"Damn, more weirdos down from the Wasatch Front."

"I gave our dining table to D.I. since we never use it."

"Excuse me, but you're blocking my sun."

Canyon of Self-Hate

"I need a trial separation that's more separate than this."

Women of the 90's

"Utah balances its environmental concerns with economic development."

"Have we forgotten anything? Yes, my sanity!"

"Do you have a dollar-night special?"

"Oh, no. Utah raptors!"

"I knew we shouldn't have left without a word of prayer."

"These dinosaurs are migrating back and forth here. . . . Why?"

The end of dinosaurs in Utah.

"We'd like to welcome our newest member who is president of a billion-dollar computer software company."